THE DECLINE AND RISE OF INSTITUTIONS

A Modern Survey of the Austrian Contribution to the Economic Analysis of Institutions

Liya Palagashvili
State University of New York, Purchase

Ennio Piano
George Mason University, Virginia

David Skarbek
King's College London

AUSTRIAN ECONOMICS

Peter Boettke

CAMBRIDGE
UNIVERSITY PRESS

Cambridge Elements ≡

CAMBRIDGE
UNIVERSITY PRESS

University Printing House, Cambridge CB2 8BS, United Kingdom

One Liberty Plaza, 20th Floor, New York, NY 10006, USA

477 Williamstown Road, Port Melbourne, VIC 3207, Australia

4843/24, 2nd Floor, Ansari Road, Daryaganj, Delhi – 110002, India

79 Anson Road, #06–04/06, Singapore 079906

Cambridge University Press is part of the University of Cambridge.

It furthers the University's mission by disseminating knowledge in the pursuit of education, learning, and research at the highest international levels of excellence.

www.cambridge.org
Information on this title: www.cambridge.org/9781316649176
DOI: 10.1017/9781108186179

First published 2017

A catalogue record for this publication is available from the British Library.

ISBN 978-1-316-64917-6 Paperback
ISSN 2399-651X (online)
ISSN 2514-3867 (print)

The Decline and Rise of Institutions

Liya Palagashvili, Ennio Piano,
and
David Skarbek

Abstract *Institutions are the formal or informal 'rules of the game' that facilitate economic, social, and political interactions. These include such things as legal rules, property rights, constitutions, political structures, and norms and customs. The main theoretical insights from Austrian economics regarding private property rights and prices, entrepreneurship, and spontaneous order mechanisms play a key role in advancing institutional economics. The Austrian economics framework provides an understanding for which institutions matter for growth, how they matter, and how they emerge and can change overtime. Specifically, Austrians have contributed significantly to the areas of institutional stickiness and informal institutions, self-governance and self-enforcing contracts, institutional entrepreneurship, and the political infrastructure for development.*

Keywords: *Austrian economics, institutional economics, political economy, economic development, emergent orders, property rights, comparative economic systems*

JEL classifications: *A33, B53, O17, P16*

Issns: *2514-3867 (print), 2399-651X (online)* **Isbns:** 9781316649176 PB, 9781108186179 OC

1 Introduction

The 1990s was the decade of the rise of institutional analysis within economic theory and history. Since those years, economists who focused on institutional analysis are now being recognized by their profession. This is attested to by the Nobel Prize committee's choice to award scholars, such as Ronald Coase in 1991, Douglass North in 1993, and Oliver Williamson and Elinor Ostrom (2009), for their contributions in economics and institutions research. This institutionalist revolution had a profound impact on the economic profession as a whole, and on the field of development economics in particular. Thanks to the institutionalist revolution, discussion on the nature of differences in economic performance across time and space moved away from the formalism of growth models, which have been unable to capture the fundamental causes of economic development, to a more comparative and historical analysis that focuses on alternative institutional arrangements (Acemoglu *et al.*, 2001; Glaeser and Shleifer 2002; Rodrik *et al.* 2004).

The rediscovery of institutions by the economic profession came after decades of institutional antisepticism. Since the 1940s, mainstream economists have focused more and more on the mathematical conditions and characteristics of equilibrium states, and while economics gained some of the elegance and clarity (at least to the initiated) of mathematics, it lost some of the most important insights of the classical economists such as Hume and Smith, as well as those of the early marginalists such as Menger, Wicksteed, Bohm-Bawerk, Wicksell, Mises, and Knight.

At the same time as the mainstream was forgetting this lesson about the importance of institutional analysis to economic reasoning, the Austrian school of economics was emerging as a distinct tradition within the profession. Up to this point, Austrian economists had been recognized within mainstream economics, although they had theoretical positions that did not perfectly coincide with those of the Anglo-Saxon and North American traditions (for example, in capital theory, interest theory, and the theory of the business cycle). But for the most part, Austrians and the other neo-classical schools saw themselves as closer to each other than to competing schools such as the old institutionalists and the Marxians. These similarities included methodology (they all saw themselves as marginalists and subjectivists), theory (their approach were all price theoretic), and a focus on processes over equilibria.

After the 1940s, with the disappearance of Marxian economics and the old institutionalists from the top universities, and with the rest of the profession taking the road of formalism, the Austrians (with a few others, Austrian influenced economists such as James Buchanan, Kenneth Boulding, and Ronald Coase) remained the only ones to combine the methodological stances of marginalism and subjectivism with a focus on processes, and, therefore, on the institutional environment within which economic action takes place. The consistent application of subjectivism, price theory, and process analysis makes the Austrian school of economics the only consistently institutional tradition in the history of modern economics.

The purpose of this paper is to survey the Austrian contribution to the economic analysis of institutions. Section 2 discusses the early development of the Austrian theory of institutional evolution and the role of institutions in the working of the market process. The Austrian position emerged and was clarified in the context of two of the most important theoretical debates in the history of the discipline: the first was the Methodenstreit, an economics controversy that took place towards the end of the nineteenth century between Carl Menger and the German Historical School; the second was the Socialist Calculation Debate of the 1920s and 1930s that took place between Mises, Hayek, and followers on the one hand and the market socialists on the other. In this section, we also discuss Hayek's re-elaboration and extension of Menger's theory of institutions and its implications for political economy. Section 3 focuses on the contemporary contribution of Austrian economists to comparative institutional analysis, and in particular the development of the Robust Political Economy paradigm. Unlike those of the earlier authors, and while deeply rooted in economic theory, the contributions of contemporary Austrian are distinctively applied. The Robust Political Economy paradigm has been successfully applied to the political economy of transition, the comparative institutional analysis of development, and the institutional arrangements of self-enforcing exchange and self-governance. Section 4 briefly concludes.

2 Austrian Economics as Institutional Economics

2.1 Carl Menger against the German Historical School

Carl Menger is the founding figure of Austrian Economics. A professor at the University of Vienna, Menger's two major contributions to economics were his reformulation of economic theory on subjectivist foundations and his writings on the methodology of economic science, and especially the relationship between economic theory and institutional analysis.

The former contribution was the focus of Menger's first book, *Principles of Economics* (Menger [1871] 2007). Here Menger argues that economic action as well as the resulting unintended consequences of such action cannot be properly understood without recognizing the role of the subjective preferences of the economic agents. Menger introduced into the German speaking world the notion that human action is aimed at the satisfaction of subjective preferences and that such preferences are never satisfied absolutely, but only at the margin. No consumer is ever faced with the choice between all the diamonds in the world and all the water in the world, but only between one more unit of diamonds and one more unit of water.

His subjective utility theory was able to solve the paradox of why the monetary value of a life-preserving resource such as water is lower than that of a luxury good such as diamonds. Since the former is more abundant than the latter, consumers value one more unit of water less than one more unit of diamonds. This counterintuitive solution is the result of the principle of diminishing marginal utility: Consumers get utility from consuming goods and services. This utility is subjective and diminishing in quantity consumed: The satisfaction enjoyed from the second of a good is, ceteris paribus, lower than that enjoyed from the first unit, that from the third unit lower than that from the second unit, and so forth. For this contribution, Menger is identified as one of the main contributors to the marginalist and subjectivist revolution in economic theory alongside Leon Walras and William Stanley Jevons.

Menger's second contribution was prompted by the reaction, within the context of the German speaking world, to his *Principles*. Until after the publication of his first work, Menger saw himself as contributing to the German school of economics. He did not expect that the most prominent figure of this school, Gustav Schmoller, would reject his approach as fundamentally incompatible with the German tradition because it made use of "the English fiction of egoistic economic man" as a theoretical foundation for the formulation of universal economic laws (Caldwell 2004: 37). Menger's response to Schmoller's criticism gave start to the first great methodological debate in the history of economic thought, the Methodenstreit.[1]

Menger's response took the form of his second book, *Investigations into the Method of the Social Sciences* (Menger [1883] 2009). In it, Menger provides a defense of the theoretical approach to economics against the more "empirical" one of the German historical schools.

---

[1] For a history of the Methodenstreit, see Caldwell (2004), and especially chapter 3.

According to the former, the pronouncements of economics are universal laws that can be derived from the subjectivist theory of value. According to the latter, on the other hand, no such thing as universal economic laws can be achieved. Thus, economists should content themselves with empirically derived generalizations of nationally and historically specific institutions.

The *Investigtions* contain two of Menger's most important contributions to economic theory and methodology. Both contributions were deeply rooted in the deductive method in the derivation of universal economic laws and of the subjective theory of value initially developed in his *Principles*. The first contribution was the revival of the spontaneous order tradition in the moral sciences. Menger's second contribution in the *Investigations* consists in the formulation of a method for the study of spontaneous social phenomena (Cowan and Rizzo 1996) in direct opposition to the "historical method" of the German School.

2.1.1 Social Institutions as Organic Social Phenomena

According to Menger, all social phenomena can be categorized as either organic or pragmatic. A pragmatic social phenomenon is the result of the purposive plan of an individual or group of individuals. The organization of a bureaucratic body or an army, the construction of a building, and so forth, are all examples of pragmatic phenomena since their features can be directly traced back to the opinions and intensions of specific individuals (a government official, a general, or an engineer) (Menger 2009: 145).

There is, though, a variety of social phenomena that cannot be explained in this way since they are not the intentional result of anyone's intention. This second category of social phenomena, Menger calls organic. Organic social phenomena have their origin in the opinions, intentions, and actions of individuals, but their specific characteristics were not designed by any human mind. Much like the features of an organism, these result from the interaction of the various parts of society, each pursuing their own individual ends, among themselves and with their environment (Menger 2009: 146). Market prices are an example of an organic social phenomenon. Individual tastes, the constraints imposed by them by others and by nature, and the resulting choices are what determine the exchange ratios (the relative prices) of all the commodities in the economy. No single individual is responsible for the precise price relations emerging in the market at any given point in time, but these reflect the actions of all the economic agents.

Menger goes beyond this organic theory of price formation and extends the argument not only to social phenomena, but also to social institutions themselves. In so doing, Menger is building on an intellectual tradition that goes back two centuries, to the works of Bernard de Mandeville, David Hume, Adam Ferguson, and Adam Smith.

The fundamental proposition of this tradition is that most social institutions are, in Adam Ferguson's words "the result of human action but not of human design" (Ferguson [1767] 1995), or, as Menger puts it "the unintended creations of the human mind, but not how they came about" (Menger 2009: 149). The laws of morality, language, money, markets, cities, and even the state, are, in Menger's view, all examples of organic institutions. Like market prices, these institutions are the result of the interaction of a multitude of individuals reciprocally adapting their behavior and plans to the behavior and plans of everyone else.

2.1.2 The Genetic-Causal Method and the Study of Institutions

Menger's view of social institutions as organic phenomena has, in his own view, fundamental implications for the methodology of the social sciences. Indeed, Menger posited that the main scope of the social sciences was to understand "How can it be that institutions which serve the common welfare and are extremely significant for its development come into being without a common will directed toward establishing them" (Menger 2009: 146).[2]

According to Menger, the historical method employed by the German school was unfit to the task. This method consisted in the accumulation of historical evidence on the characteristic institutions of different societies across time and space and their explanation by means of analogy (Menger 2009: 144). The members of the German school rejected methodological individualistic explanations because of its assumed incompatibility with a "unified view of ... social structures." This rejection prevents them from achieving an "exact understanding" of these institutions, and forces them to appeal to allusions of unexplored processes of natural development (Menger 2009: 150).

---

[2] Italics in the original.

Furthermore, the historical method is severely limited when it comes to social institutions that originated in the distant past, given the impossibility to accumulate reliable empirical evidence. A follower of the historical method is therefore left with theoretically uninformed inferences based on the little available evidence (Menger 2009: 224).

In his book, Menger proposes an alternative method for the study of institutions, one rooted in marginalist economic theory. Cowan and Rizzo (1996) refer to it as the "genetic–causal" method. In their rendition, the genetic–causal method relies on three pillars for the explanation of social phenomena. Agents in society act purposefully to achieve their subjectively chosen goals; the actions of these agents have a causal relationship with the overall, emergent social outcome; and, finally, this causal relationship takes the form of a process from actions to outcomes (Cowan and Rizzo 1996: 273, 295).

A genetic–causal explanation of social phenomena differs from a simple claim of functional dependence or one of logical implication. While the latter can, and should be part of the explanation, they do not exhaust it as long as the process from purposeful actions to unintended outcomes is left unspecified (Cowan and Rizzo 1996: 292–296). In modern jargon, in order to make sense of a social institution, the discussion of the functional significance of an institutional arrangement within the context of society is not enough: a theory of the origin of the institutions themselves has to be provided. Furthermore, this theory has to be compatible with the assumptions of instrumental rationality and incentive compatibility.

In the Investigations, Menger provides two examples of a social scientific explanation consistent with the genetic–causal method. The first, and arguably most famous one, is his theory of the function and origin of money. Against other theories that see the state as the originator of money as a means of exchange and store of value, Menger argued that money emerged out of a barter economy as the result of a process consistent with the self-interest of the agents in the economy. In a barter economy, the extent of mutually beneficial exchange is limited by the requirement of a double coincidence of wants between the two parties. An entrepreneurial agent finds out that she can reduce the costs associated with exchange by carrying with her a good that she knows to be widely desired by others. Theory and empirical evidence both suggest that this good will have some physical and economic characteristics such as being easy to carry around, resistant to bad weather, and that can maintain its use value for a relatively long period of time. Guided by their own economic advantage, other individuals follow suit, until the entire economy ends up adopting the good as a widely accepted medium of exchange (Menger 2009: 155).[3]

The second example in Menger's Investigations is his theory of the state and the origins of the law. According to Menger, legal theory is a particularly fit object of study of the genetic–causal method. Menger reintroduced the distinction, already clear in the writings of the Scottish moral philosophers of the Eighteenth century, between state-made law, what he refers to as "statutes," and spontaneously emerged law. The latter tend to be characterized by a deeper conformity with "the particular conditions of the population from whose mind law originated" (Menger 2009: 228). Similarities across times and cultures in human societies are therefore due to some universal features of mankind, while the many differences are due to the specific needs and characteristics of these societies.

In Menger's opinion, "[L]aw as the intended result of the will of an organized national community or of its rulers is a phenomenon which does not challenge the sagacity of the scholar unduly either in respect of its general nature or its origin." (Menger 2009: 223). More interesting is the case of those laws that, although the result of an "unreflective" process, lead to socially beneficial outcomes.[4] Unfortunately, Menger's legal theory and the underlying theory of the state, although insightful, fail to remain faithful to his own methodological principles. Thus, Menger assumes that the emergence of the state can be explained away by simply pointing out that it is in the interest of every individual to establish an impartial arbiter, the state, to impose the respect of the law to all members of society. Since "[w]hat benefits all, or at least the far greater majority, gradually is realized by all": the emergence of a state, the purpose of which is the limitation of "individual despotism" is only "a natural consequence" (Menger 2009: 225–226). Menger's explanation fails to consider the collective action

---

[3] It's noteworthy to point out that Menger's explanation does not content itself with describing the beneficial function of money for society as a whole, but provides a credible story for how it emerged in the first place.

[4] These Mengerian themes will be at the center of Hayek's own legal and institutional theory.

problem, that is, the incentive compatibility constraint, of a movement from anarchy to the centralized enforcement of the law.[5]

2.2 The Socialist Calculation Debate and the Rise of Institutionally Antiseptic Economics

Since the marginalist revolution in the 1870s, the Austrian School was seen as an integral part of the neoclassical mainstream alongside the School of Lausanne, with its focus on the conditions for a general equilibrium that could be described in terms of a system of equations, and the British School, with its emphasis on partial equilibrium and comparative statics. The members of the Austrian school themselves tended to emphasize the common grounds between them and the Swiss and British fellow marginalists in opposition to those alternative schools of thought that refuted the subjective theory of value and marginal analysis, such as the Marxians, the German historicists, and the American institutionalists (Mises [1933] 2003).

At the turn of the 1940s, the same Austrian scholars would reach a very different assessment. This change was the result of the socialist calculation debate, one of the most important debates within the economic profession in the history of the discipline. Started by the publication of Mises's groundbreaking paper on the impossibility of rational economic calculation (Mises [1920] 1990), the debate lasted for almost two decades and saw the participation of the major figures within the economic profession, including Frank H. Knight (1936), Abba P. Lerner (1934–1935, 1937), Oskar Lange (1936–1937), and Joseph Schumpeter ([1942] 2008).

This debate is of foremost importance in the development of the Austrian school and of the history of economic thought in general for two reasons. First, it forced the Austrians to articulate their process perspective, as opposed to the static, "equilibrium,"perspective of the Walrasian and British schools (Kirzner 1988). Second, it saw the emergence, and by the beginning of the 1940s, success of an "institutionally antiseptic" economics (Boettke 2000a).[6]

---

[5] For a discussion of this collective action problem, see Tullock (1974). Theories of the emergence and evolution of a state that are in fact compatible with the genetic-causal method can be found in Olson (1993) and North *et al.* (2009).

[6] The definitive treatment of the socialist calculation debate is Lavoie ([1985] 2015). Boettke (2000b) contains all the major contributions to the debate.

2.2.1 Mises's Impossibility Theorem

Mises published his "Economic Calculation in the Socialist Commonwealth" in 1920, two years after the soviet regime introduced the set of policies known as war communism in the USSR. The central argument of this paper is what can be called Mises's Impossibility Theorem: under a system of communal ownership of the means of production, the rational economic allocation of resources among competing uses is impossible. Mises's argument must be read as a direct criticism of the theoretical framework underlying the economic experiment of the Soviet Regime, that is the theory of the "natural economy" developed by Marx (1938) and further elaborated by Lenin (1920) and Bukharin (1979). According to this theory, once the capitalist mode of production had been reached, the world would be dominated by one gigantic monopolist, which would then be easily taken over by the state, now the representative of the interests of the proletariat. This state would therefore gain control of all the physical means of production (land and capital), while labor would be free from alienation, thus spurring an unprecedented burst in productivity and the end of the economic problem, that is, scarcity (Prychitko 2008). The new socialist regime would therefore out-compete capitalism on every margin: fairness, productivity, and satisfaction of consumers' wants.

Mises's response to these claims was that, in a socialist commonwealth extending over the entirety of the human race and in which all economic resources are controlled by a central planning authority, the rational (economic) allocation of resources is impossible. In his argument, Mises makes two extreme concessions to the opposing side of the argument. First, Mises assumes that the central planner possesses complete information about technology and the tastes of the consumers. Second, Mises assumes that the planner faces no incentive problem. Finally, Mises concedes the possibility of a market for consumer goods. Once the citizens of the socialist commonwealth receive their claims against their shares of the total product of the economy (measured in "units" of value contributed to the socialist cause), they can allocate these claims among the consumer goods as they please. These claims and the goods purchased can then be freely exchanged at the spontaneously emerged market prices. In order for the socialist commonwealth to be truly identified as such, though, no market for the means of production can be in place, these must remain "res extra commercium"

(Mises [1920] 1990: 5)[7]: The allocation of resources among production processes must be the task of the central authority.

If all the conditions above are satisfied, rational economic calculation is impossible. Mises discusses the implication of his theorem under two alternative conditions. The first case is that of a static state of affairs. In a static economy, the market process has exhausted its purpose: all gains from trade have been exploited and the optimality conditions for a rational allocation of resources have been met. In other words, the market has solved the imputation problem. If a socialist regime were to take control of the commanding heights of such a society Mises concedes, we would have a socialist economy in which resources are rationally allocated.

The paradox, though, is that the socialist regime itself is not responsible for such an allocation, and therefore the logical possibility of this state of affairs is not a proof that rational economic planning is possible under socialism. Furthermore, the very assumption of a completely static economy would prevent any reallocation of the initial endowment according to egalitarian principles. Such a reallocation would in fact lead to a radical change in the economy-wide optimality conditions. Thus, even if no further change were to occur, the regime would find itself with the impossible task of replicating the market process in order to reallocate resources efficiently.

The second case analyzed by Mises is that of a dynamic state of affairs. A dynamic economy is characterized by constant change in its parameters: consumers' tastes, technology, the supply of original factors, ideas, and so forth. Under these conditions, the newly established socialist regime could not even rely on the allocation and relative prices achieved by the market process up to that point, since they would have already become obsolete. Because of its inability to rationally calculate under static conditions, the planning authority would be "groping in the dark" under dynamic conditions – the result of centralized planning would be chaos rather than the harmonious and ordered society depicted by Marx and his followers.

2.2.2 The Debate

The publication of Mises's paper and of *Socialism: An Economic and Sociological Analysis* (Mises [1922] 1981) had a profound impact on

---

[7] Italics in the original.

the economic theory and practice of socialism. The response to his argument took two forms. First, it forced socialist economists to recognize the limitations of Marx's theoretical frameworks as a guide to central planning. Mises was right in pointing out that labor does not provide an objective measure of value and is therefore of no use in the rational allocation of resources. If a socialist society is to be efficiently organized, it has to conform to the optimality conditions discovered by marginalist economic theory: that is, whenever possible, price must be equated to marginal cost. Because of their adherence to marginalist economics, their appreciation of the function of prices, and the opinion that the socialist economy should attempt to emulate (and, in doing so, outperform) the market economy, Dickinson, Lange, Lerner, Taylor, and other "market socialists" were radically distancing themselves from orthodox Marxians.

The second form of the response was not as sympathetic. In the view of the market socialists, Mises's impossibility theorem was ill-founded. There is nothing, in the mathematical theory of general equilibrium that prevents a hypothetical central planner from being able to allocate resources according to the equimarginal principle. The error of Marxian economics was not that it relied on the central planner for the allocation of resources, but that it failed to replace the consumers as the originators of the evaluation of economic resources in the model. Once the central planning authority is specified as taking the place of the consumers, the formal model of the competitive market can be used to solve the imputation problem and as a guide to the rational allocation of resources (Lerner 1934–1935: 55).

The market socialist response is symptomatic of a misunderstanding of Mises's argument. Mises never claimed that economic theory does not apply to socialism, nor that the conditions sufficient for an efficient equilibrium under socialism are different from those of a decentralized market. Mises instead argued that under dynamic circumstances, the absence of a market for the factors of production prevents the emergence of meaningful market prices as guide to the action of producers and entrepreneurs. Without market prices, producers are prevented from translating the preferences of the consumers into valuations of the factors of production. This problem of value imputation from goods of lower order (consumer goods) to goods of higher order (capital, natural resources, and labor) is what, in a market economy, drives resources towards their most valued uses. In a market economy, each entrepreneur has some expectation about the condition of market demand in the foreseeable future. Based on these expectations and the profit and loss calculation,[8] entrepreneurs bid against each other for the control of the goods of higher order. After the production process has been completed, the plans of the entrepreneurs are tested against the actual conditions of the market.

In the late 1930s and early 1940s, F. A. Hayek took upon himself the task of elaborating a response to the market socialist "solution" to Mises's impossibility theorem. Hayek's stance can be summarized as follows. First, Hayek stressed the fundamental difference between the technological and the economic problem.[9] Second, the Austrian economist refuted the market-socialist position by stressing that the knowledge that planners would need to employ in their decision-making is dispersed. The price system that operates in markets, by contrast, economizes on the amount of information that actors have to process in order to coordinate their decisions. More importantly, though, this economic knowledge is embedded in the process of price formation in the competitive market process. It is not the case that setting the "right" price would retrieve the "right" knowledge to engage in rational economic calculation, but rather that the knowledge can only emerge in the process of exchange, and it ceases to exist without it. In socialist economies where private ownership is banned, firm managers would be unable to set the correct prices because the process of exchange, and the prices that emerge from exchange, do not exist. The institutional setting undermines the ability for decentralized information about the relative scarcity of resources to emerge, thus undermining rational economic calculation. Hayek explains (1940: 196):

> What is forgotten is that the method which under given condition is the cheapest is a thing which has to be discovered, and to be discovered anew, sometimes almost from day to day, by the entrepreneur, and that in spite of the strong inducement, it is by no means regularly the established entrepreneur, the man in charge of the existing plant, who will discover what is the best method.

---

[8] The entrepreneur will only buy up until the present discounted marginal value product of the resource is greater than the marginal cost.

[9] Hayek further elaborated this point in a series of lectures at the University of Virginia two decades later (Hayek [1961] 2014).

Thus, the advantages of competitive market systems are tied to the existence of markets, and replacing competitive markets will subsequently eliminate the process of competition, knowledge discovery, and emergence of prices that signal relative scarcities.

Hayek further elaborated these concepts in *The Use of Knowledge in Society*, which has come to be regarded as his most important contribution to economic theory (Hayek 1945). In this paper, Hayek argues that the economists' focus on the mathematical conditions for a stable competitive equilibrium (as well as the welfare properties of the latter) prevented them from a full appreciation of the coordinating role played by the price mechanism in achieving such an equilibrium. The mathematical approach to general equilibrium, though necessarily correct from a logical point of view, is unable to describe the causal mechanism that brings about a general increase in the mutual consistency of the plans of all the agents in the economy. In elaborating and pursuing these plans, individuals act upon their knowledge of the underlying conditions of the economy (the tastes of all consumers, the existing technology, the supply and demand of natural resources and capital goods, and so forth).

Given the imperfection of the human mind, this knowledge is never objectively accurate or exhaustive. Indeed, as Hayek pointed out, this knowledge is by its very nature contextual[10] and subjective, and therefore cannot be easily collected and utilized by a central authority. Only a decentralized market can make the best use of this knowledge, but, even more fundamentally, only a decentralized market can generate this knowledge and incentivize people to adjust to it in a way that increases the mutual consistency of the plans of the agents in the economy.

This process of adjustment is made possible by the price system. In making their decisions about buying and selling, saving and investing, individuals look at market prices. These prices convey information and knowledge about the underlying economic conditions (that is, the relative scarcity of economic resources) of the market. An increase in the price of a good leads to the marginal buyers to refrain from consuming it, without any need to know the causes of such an increase. The market process thus leads to the allocation of resources

---

[10] In Hayek's words: "The knowledge of the particular circumstances of time and place" ([1945] 1948: 80).

towards their most valued uses without anyone in the economy knowing what these uses are.

Since the knowledge held by the individuals is subjective and limited, there is no a priori reason to believe that this knowledge is ever going to be correct. The price system (which relies on the feedback mechanism of profits and losses) leads to an adjustment of this knowledge and, as a consequence, of the individual plans that rely upon it. Economic losses signal to the firm that the knowledge and expectations on which its plan was based might be incorrect. For example, the firm might have overestimated the demand of its output from consumers, meaning that it was using an inefficient amount of factors of production. The firm can (although not all firms at all times immediately will) adjust to this newly discovered knowledge and reduce the level of output, thus freeing factors for more valued uses.

As the discussion above exemplifies, the Austrian position as expressed by Mises and Hayek during the socialist calculation debate is essentially a comparative institutional one. The difference between a market economy and a socialist one lies not in the difference between the actors that populate them, but rather in the institutional environment that characterizes each of them. A market economy is one in which the property rights arrangement is itself the product of a spontaneous process of discovery, serves a fundamental role in generating a process of rivalry among alert entrepreneurs. In turn, this process leads to the emergence of relative prices, which guide the actions of the entrepreneurs in allocating resources efficiently among competing uses. On the other hand, a socialist economy is defined by the absence of property rights over the means of production. This institutional difference leads to the absence of a price system, which in turn leads to the impossibility of rational economic allocation of resources. Some actors trying to pursue the same goal (rational allocation of resources), achieve a different result due the epistemic feature of the institutional environment within which they behave.

Kirzner (1973) advanced this understanding of resources being redirected from lower-valued to higher-valued uses through the entrepreneur attempting to exploit previously unnoticed profit opportunities, thereby reducing price differentials and allowing the system as a whole to move towards equilibrium. Thus, these profits (and losses) are feedback mechanisms regarding the allocation of resources, and they also incentivize entrepreneurs to discover new opportunities for production and innovation. This entrepreneurial action is guided by relative price signals and profits, and these signals come about through exchange made possible by property rights. Property rights are the key foundation here because they incentivize individuals to recognize the most-valued uses of their property, and, in doing so, reveal the values they place on the property through voluntary exchange.

As we discuss below, the Austrian framework has been used to analyze the Soviet economy and its massive problems with shortages and poverty. Because the Soviet firms were unable to engage in rational economic calculation and unable to use real market prices for decision-making, this led to misallocations and waste of resources, shortages in most industries, substantial black market activity, and the stifling of productive entrepreneurship and innovation. It is the institution of property rights that generate growth-enhancing processes such as entrepreneurship, technological discoveries, and movements toward greater efficiency in production.

The focus on the functional significance of property rights in the market economy is one of the most important contributions from the Austrian framework as it explains the process through which the role of property rights, prices, and entrepreneurship leads to growth and wealth in societies. In this way, Austrian economics is directly linked to both institutional and development economics because it offers a framework for understanding the wealth of nations and how institutional arrangements can lead to growth by influencing decision-making through shaping incentives and impacting the flow of information.

2.3 Law, Legislation, and Social Order

In the aftermath of the socialist calculation debate, Hayek's intellectual journey slowly moved away from the abstraction of theoretical economics to a broader set of topics, from the history of social scientific thought (Hayek [1952a] 1980) to theoretical psychology (Hayek [1952b] 1976), but most importantly to the realm of political philosophy and political economy broadly understood. Hayek would keep reformulating the governing principles of a free society from a classical liberal political economy perspective from the 1940s to the end of his life. In *The Constitution of Liberty*, Hayek ([1960] 1978) attempts to revive this tradition by appealing to the work of such authors as David Hume and Adam Smith, the American Founding Fathers, Alexis de Tocqueville and Lord Acton, and his own mentor Ludwig von Mises.

One important theme of the book is the theoretical analysis of the institutional framework needed for a society of free and responsible individuals to persist and prosper (Hayek 1960: 215–231). Hayek expanded this analysis in the three volumes of his next work, *Law, Legislation, and Liberty*. In particular, the first volume – titled *Rules and Order* – is dedicated to the issue of the institutional foundations of social order (Hayek 1973). This work can be interpreted as an elaboration and clarification of some themes already explored by Carl Menger.

The main focus of the book is the distinction between social orders. In Hayek's understanding, order is a necessary condition for the very existence of society. This insight is not, of course, original to Hayek, but goes back to classical, medieval, and early modern thinkers. Hayek's contribution was that of identifying the epistemological origins of the necessity of order for the functioning of society. He also recognized that social order can take different forms, which fall into two broader categories: made orders and grown or spontaneous orders (Hayek 1973: 35). These orders differ in the principles by which the elements that compose them interact with one another. It is the scope of the social sciences to identify these principles to be able to make predictions about the behavior of the individual agents, as well as that of the entirety of the order itself.

In a made order, the coordination among the elements that compose it is realized by ex ante providing each one of them with specific instructions about the actions to take under a variety of circumstances. Each element occupies a role within the broader order, and the necessary actions are all aimed at the realization of a well-specified goal. Thus, we can characterize a made order as "artificial" or "exogenous." The exogeneity of the order is given by the fact that the order is not a result of the reciprocal adjustment of plans and behavior of the individual members of the group; that is, it does not emerge out of the interaction of the individuals but is instead determined by an authority that precedes and is outside the order itself. In the context of society, organizations are a made order, since they are established with a given purpose, and membership requires the fulfillment of specified tasks; all of which are necessary if the organization if to realize its goals.

A classic example of artificial order is the business firm.[11] The manager of the firm is instructed by the owner to maximize profits; the realization of which required the manager to hire workers who will then be required to complete certain tasks. Within the context of the firm, interactions among the employees, those between the employees and the manager, and between the employees and the manager and the physical environment is specified in their contracts. Assuming away the problem of monitoring and enforcement, the behavior of the employees and the resulting order can only be understood as the product of the plan designed by the management.

In order to better identify made or exogenous orders, Hayek uses the Greek word *Taxis*. Within the context of a Taxis, order is guaranteed by the fact that its elements abide by rules that have specific characteristics. Hayek refers to this type of rule as *Thesis*. A Thesis consists in a command: it specifies the goals (the ends) and actions (the means) that an individual must adopt if the Taxis is to remain ordered and achieve its purpose.

In Hayek's view, in the social sciences, spontaneous orders occupy a more important role than made orders. In fact, the social scientific exercise is only relevant as it studies spontaneous orders. Even in the study of made orders, the focus of the social scientist revolves around those features of the organizational structure that emerge in response to the fact that organizations exist within a broader, spontaneous social context, or to counteract limitations of the commands to effectively guide the behavior of the members of the organization (Hayek 1973: 37).

While we can perceive the causes of a made order, that is, we can easily identify the causal relationship between the rules that regulate it and the concrete features of the resulting order, the same is not true of spontaneous orders. That is why social science, and not just direct observation, is needed in order to understand their functioning. This impossibility results from the major difference between a made and a spontaneous order. Unlike the former, the latter cannot serve any specific end or purpose, and as soon as some goals are imposed upon it, it either fails or ceases to be a spontaneous order. The more complex the order, the less the social scientist will be able to make accurate

---

[11] Other popular examples are the household, bureaucracies, governments, armies, and orchestras.

predictions about its concrete features. From a policy point of view, this means that the more complex the social order we want to obtain or preserve, the more we have to rely on rules rather than discretionary governance. The only way to preserve a complex order is not by trying to direct the actions of its individual agents, but by enforcing and imposing the rules on which it relies (Hayek 1973: 50–51). A spontaneous order has no purpose of its own. It is not the result of the plan of one mind or a group of minds. It is instead brought about by the purposeful interaction of a multitude of agents and organizations, each with its own objectives and ends. Such an order can therefore be characterized as relatively complex and, more importantly, abstract. A spontaneous order or, as Hayek refers to it, a Cosmos, is an abstract one in the sense that it follows abstract rules and its properties can only be perceived by abstracting from its specific features.

For a spontaneous order to emerge, the behavior of its elements has to be coordinated. Without a central authority dictating such behavior, coordination is achieved by rule-following behavior. Hayek refers to the typology of rules characteristic of a spontaneous order as Nomos. A Nomos can, but need not be, itself the result of a spontaneous process, but, in Hayek's opinion, successful historical spontaneous orders often rely on spontaneously emerged rules of just conduct, such as the Common Law in Medieval and Modern England (Hayek 1973: 45).[12]

The distinction between Nomos and Thesis can be used to understand the difference in nature and effects of "law" and "legislation." According to Hayek, the former term used to refer exclusively to those products of parliamentary decision-making that presented very specific characteristics. To be recognized as such, a law would have to "consist of rules regulating the conduct of persons towards others, applicable to an unknown number of future instances and containing prohibitions delimiting the boundary of the protected domain of each person (or organized group of persons)" (Hayek 1973: 122).

Legislation as a legal category diverges from the law in that a law cannot be "carried out." Since it is not a command specifying the actions to be undertaken in a given situation, a law "merely delimits the limits of

---

[12] "Society can . . . exist only if by a process of selection rules ave evolved which lead individuals to behave in a manner whicih makes social life possible For a rule to lead to such an order, the only requirement is that it presents the characteristics of general applicability and abstractness" (Hayek 1973: 44).

the range of permitted action and usually does not determine a particular action" (Hayek 1973: 127). A legislation, or statute, is also the product of the legislature, but used to refer only to those commands regulating the behavior of governmental and administrative agencies that are the body of a state (Hayek 1973: 137). In the last two centuries, Hayek claims, this distinction has been lost, and parliaments and legislatures have extended the dominion of legislation and statutes beyond the boundary of the public section towards the regulation of private and economic behavior. Contemporary economic policy is nothing else than the attempt of governmental agencies to dictate to private firms and consumers what to produce, how to produce it, and in what quantity, as well as the way in which it is advertised, bought, and sold (Hayek 1973: 139–140). The origin of this shift toward the governmental control of the economy via legislation was justified as a well-intentioned attempt to make society more just by imposing the principle of equality of results (or, in its weaker version, equality of opportunities) upon society, thus necessarily abandoning the liberal principle of equality before the law.

3 Toward a Genuine Institutional Economics: The Robust Political Economy Paradigm

One of the major developments within contemporary Austrian Political Economy has been the development of the Robust Political Economy Paradigm.[13] This paradigm is the result of the combination of the analytical tools developed within Austrian economics (the subjectivist methodological foundations and the focus on the process towards equilibrium rather than the mathematical conditions of the equilibrium itself) with those of other schools of thought emerged within economics since the 1950s. These schools of thought are Public Choice (Buchanan and Tullock [1962] 2004), the Property Rights School (Alchian 1965; Demsetz 1967; Alchian and Demsetz 1973), the Transaction Cost paradigm (Coase 1959, 1960), the New Institutional Economics (North 1981, 1990, 2005), and the Institutional Analysis of Development Paradigm (Ostrom 1990; Crawford and Ostrom 1995).

---

[13] This paradigm was first introduced in Boettke (1993, 2001) and Boettke and Leeson (2004). Pennington (2011) explores the implications of the paradigm for political philosophy and public policy.

Boettke (2012) refers to the exponents of these schools as the "mainline" of economics; that is, those scholars who do not just practice economics, but do so within the analytical tradition of Adam Smith. The combination of these schools results in a comparative institutional paradigm that focuses on the rationale of alternative institutional arrangements as well as on their consequences for economic performance. Notwithstanding the obvious differences, these schools have much in common. They are all build on strong price theoretic foundations, have an intellectual debt towards the Austrian school, Mises and Hayek in particular (Boettke 2012), and, more importantly, put the rules of the game of society at the center front of the analysis.

Public Choice, the application of rational choice theory to the realm of politics, was pioneered by political economists of the caliber of James Buchanan, Gordon Tullock, and Mancur Olson. Public choice theorists have mostly dealt with two subject matters: the theory of the decision-making process for the rules of the game of society (the constitutional level of analysis, or constitutional political economy (Buchanan 1987)) and the modeling of the behavior of individuals within those rules (the study of political behavior proper, from the theory of voting to that of regulation, from the analysis of rent-seeking to that of autocratic governance, and so forth).

As the name suggests, the Property Rights tradition focuses on the role of ownership arrangements within an economic system. Indeed, according to the members of this school the very discipline of economics consists in the study of property rights arrangements. These arrangements are the major determinants of the incentive structure faced by economic agents and therefore have a huge impact on the performance of the economy as a whole. When property rights are defined and enforced efficiently, individuals internalize the benefits and costs of their actions, which in turn incentivize them to make the best use of the resources available in the economy.

Another important contribution of the property rights paradigm was the provision of a theoretical explanation of the evolution of property right arrangements from communal property rights to individualized ones. According to this explanation, rights will spontaneously adjust to changing benefits and costs. The classic example is that of land ownership among Native American tribes. Before the arrival of the Europeans, land was commonly owned among these tribes and because hunting was done on such a small scale, the cost of enforcement of individualized property rights would be too high relative to the benefits of reducing the potential negative effects on the stock of beavers. However, as the fur trade with Western Europe became one of the biggest sources of income for these tribes, the potential cost of over-hunting bacame so high as to make individualized land ownership efficient. Thus, contrary to the popular opinion, property rights can emerge to reconcile private and social costs and benefits (Alchian and Demsetz 1973).[14]

Ronald Coase is rightfully identified as responsible for some of the most important developments within economics in the twentieth century. Coase's colleague at Chicago, George Stigler (1992), once wrote in the field of law and economics, there is a B.C. and A.C., a "Before Coase" and an "After Coase." This can perhaps be said about Coase's influence in the field of transaction cost economics. In his paper on the "nature of the firm", Coase (1937) identifies the existence of costs associated with the use of the price mechanism of an unhampered market economy as the principle cause for the emergence of organizations such as firms for the coordination of production. This paper had an important role in directing the attention of economists to the study of organizations, and of firms in particular, which is one of the major focuses of analysis of the so-called New Institutional Economics (Klein 1999; Williamson 2002).

Coase explored and further extended his insight on the relevance of transaction costs for the organization of real-world markets later in his career (Coase 1959, 1960). In these papers, Coase formulates what would become known as the "Coase theorem"[15]. According to this theorem, in the absence of transaction costs (that is, if the costs of creation and enforcement of property rights and contracts are null), the presence of external economies will not lead to inefficiency. As property rights over all aspects of the use of resources are perfectly specified, individuals will bargain over these rights until they have been allocated to their most valued uses.

Although the contribution of the Coase theorem to the clarification of the problem of externality and social cost is of great importance, Coase himself believed that the major insight of the two papers was to direct economists' attention to those cases (which, in his opinion, were the

---

[14] For a modern restatement of the property rights approach and a variety of applications, see Barzel (1997).

[15] For a critical discussion of the Coase theorem, see Medema and Zerbe (1999).

overwhelming majority) characterized by positive transaction costs. If, according to the Coase theorem, the final allocation of rights over resources is independent of the initial allocation under the assumption of positive transaction costs this is no longer the case. Alternative institutional environments will therefore have different effects on the efficiency of market processes. The focus of economic analysis should be that of studying these alternative arrangements and their net effects on the working of the economy. In Coase's own words:

> A better approach [than the one proposed by standard welfare economic theory] would seem to be to start our analysis with a situation approximating that which actually exists, to examine the effects of a proposed policy change and to attempt to decide whether the new situation would be, in total, better or worse than the original one ... But in choosing between social arrangements within the context of which individual decisions are made, we have to bear in mind that a change in the existing system which will lead to an improvement in some decisions may well lead to a worsening of others.   *(Coase 1960: 43–44)*

Because of passages like the one above, Ronald Coase is also identified as the intellectual father of the New Institutional Economics (NIE). In the last three decades, though, the NIE framework has been mostly associated with the work of economist and economic historian Douglass North. North's theoretical and applied work putinstitutional analysis back at the center front of the academic conversation. In his *Structure and Change in Economic History* (North 1981), North poses a radical challenge to neoclassical economics. Because of the focus on equilibrium conditions, standard economics had demonstrated itself to be incapable of understanding economic change, that is the change in the performance of economies through time. In order to achieve this goal, a new paradigm had to be developed.

This paradigm is fundamentally economic in that it does not assume away the problem of scarcity (incentives do matter) and is methodologically individualistic (historical processes are determined by, and do not determine, individual behavior), but within a context of positive transaction costs. Thus, the focus has to be on institutions and, even more importantly, on institutional "change." According to North, a theory of economic change is (or, better, ought to be) a theory of institutional change. Such a theory consists of three parts: a theory of property rights, a theory of the state, and a theory of ideology

(North 1981: 7). Property rights determine the incentive structure faced by the agents within society, and therefore the allocation pattern of the economic resources of society, while the theory of the state studies the enforcement of these rights. According to North, these two are necessary but not sufficient. A theory of the formation and change of the belief system of society is also needed, since it affects both the content and enforcement of property rights and can operate as a binding constraint on the actions of the state.

North further elaborated this theory of institutions in his *Institutions, Institutional Change, and Economic Performance* (North 1990). The book has since become a classic. In it, North formulated the standard definition of institutions as "the rules of the game of society or, more formally . . . the humanly devised constraint that shape human interaction" (North 1990: 3). The function of institutions is to reduce the amount of uncertainty that every individual possesses about others' behavior. The individuals of the model are not assumed as possessing perfect understanding of the physical and social world, but rather "subjectively derived models that diverge among individuals" (North 1990: 17). By introducing predictability of behavior, that is, by increasing the reciprocal consistency of the variety of subjective mental models of the members of society, institutions allow for an ordered pattern of human interaction in production and exchange.

North's focus is thus on institutions as both facilitating and constraining human action. The specific characteristics of the resulting order will depend on the underlying institutional framework of society.

As institutions reward more some classes of behavior, these would be relatively more common, with obvious consequences for the overall performance of the economy. By determining the incentive structure of the economy, institutions lead to the formation of organizations, groups of individuals with some common interest coming together in order to realize a specified objective. Organizations will in fact attempt to preserve some institutions, wipe out others, and introduce new ones. Thus, in North's account, organizations play a central role in the evolution of institutions and, therefore, in economic change and performance through time.

The Institutional Analysis of Development paradigm studies how different institutional arrangements can impact community solutions and the self-governing capacities of people. Institutions can influence individuals' payoffs for engaging in community solutions, but they can also influence certain beliefs and cultures and thus may suppress self-governing capacities and civil society. The IAD framework was developed by political scientists Vincent and Elinor Ostrom. Polycentricity is a fundamental theme in the work of the Ostroms (V. Ostrom 1999; E. Ostrom 2010).[16]

Polycentricism and federalism have been identified as key structures here because they rely on Tiebout competition to align incentives between the principal (the citizens) and the agent (the political authority). In a traditional federalist structure, the exit power that citizens have places checks on the levels of local government when they renege on their contractual agreements. Because citizens can locate elsewhere and thus lower levels of government will compete for residents by enforcing the contractual obligations between the two. Federalist structures have obvious limits though, one of them being that although sub-government contracts with their citizens are self-enforcing, the contract that individuals have with the national government is not. This means that national governments can choose to limit the powers or number of sub-governments and effectively break the federalist structure. Polycentricism describes a system with many centers of decision-making units that are formally independent of each other, which involves multiple, overlapping systems of autonomous governments. Vincent and Elinor Ostrom have discussed how the competition between governments in polycentrism can align the incentives of leaders to be accountable to their people. When there are multiple competing levels of local government, it allows citizens the opportunity to "vote with their feet." The Ostroms argue that this mechanism is an important feature of polycentricism in US public economies that aligned the incentives of individuals to government leaders and encouraged local governments and agencies to be more accountable to their citizens.

Vincent Ostrom's theoretical work on polycentric orders utilizes this approach and is closely connected with Hayek's knowledge processes and spontaneous order mechanisms. Vincent describes polycentric systems as institutions that are able to produce and convey information

---

[16] For a detailed discussion on the connection between the Ostroms and Austrian economics, see Boettke *et al.* (2014). This paper discusses both how the Ostroms were influenced by Austrian economics and how the Ostroms' works can influence the Austrian research agenda

and cope with uncertainty. He highlights that polycentricism gives significant autonomy to communities so they can test different rules, and this experimentation allows for the exchange of local knowledge and enables important feedback mechanisms. When individuals pursue their own interests, they are constantly engaged in a process of learning and discovery – individuals draw upon the knowledge and skills of others as a complement to the limits that prevail in the competence of each individual (V. Ostrom 1982; in Aligica and Boettke 2009, 69). V. Ostrom stresses that the primary function of institutions is piecing together relevant information, the "local knowledge," that is dispersed among actors. This information is relevant because other individuals depend upon it, and it this piecing of local knowledge that is needed for societies to function. The exchange of information and knowledge are crucial features of complex social orders and the role of institutions is to facilitate the "elucidation and transmission of information so that human beings can constructively take account of one another's interests as they interact with each other" (V. Ostrom 1980: 311). Within a polycentric system, local knowledge and norms that are constantly changing and developing are exactly the mechanisms of spontaneous order that is at work and that allow for a range of learning and discovery.

Elinor Ostrom's major contribution to political economy consisted in the application of the IAD framework to the study of the provision of common pool resources by self-governing communities across the world (E. Ostrom 1990). Against the traditional wisdom regarding collective action situations (Olson 1965), which predicts "collective inaction," that is, that the group will be unable to organize effectively, Elinor Ostrom provided theory and evidence of the contrary. Self-governing communities can, given the presence of eight design principles, effectively organize the provision of common pool resources around formal and informal institutions.

The development of the robust political economy paradigm has produced a sizable number of contributions in political economy. All these contributions share common methodological and theoretical foundations at the intersection of Austrian economics and the schools discussed above, as well as the focus on comparative and institutional analysis, from the study of the political economy of Soviet economic policy to the institutional framework of self-enforcing exchange and self-governance throughout history.

3.1 Soviet Socialism and the Problem of Transition

Boettke's work on the political economy of Soviet Socialism in the 1910s and 1920s (Boettke 1990), as well as his work on the problem of economic policy reform and transition in Soviet Russia in the 1980s and 1990s (Boettke 1993; 2001) makes him a forerunner of the robust political economy paradigm.

In *The Political Economy of Soviet Socialism*, Boettke offers a revisionist economic history of the early decades of economic policy in the Soviet Union. Against the standard interpretation, Boettke (1990) argues that the so-called "War Communism" was not a necessary response by Lenin and his government to the economic difficulties posed by the consequences of the first world conflict or just the necessary step towards the industrialization of Russia, but rather the first consistent experiment with Marxian socialism – the planning of the whole economy by a central authority controlling all the means of production in society. Thus, the introduction of the New Economic Policy in 1921 is not to be read as the necessary evolution of Lenin's economic policy towards a true and humane socialism. Instead, it was the necessary reaction to the realization of the failure of central planning, thus corroborating Mises's and Hayek's theoretical insight into the impossibility of rational economic calculation.

In *Why Perestroika Failed* and *Calculation and Coordination*, he also provides an alternative account of the failure of economic reform attempted by Gorbachev, which eventually led to the demise of the Soviet Union, as well as the failure of post-Soviet Russia to transit from a rent-seeking society – the economic system Russia evolved into in the decades following the death of Stalin – towards a free-market economy and from an autocratic political system to a liberal-democratic one. In Boettke's analysis, one of the main causes of these failures was the difficulty of the Soviet regime to credibly commit to its stated objectives.

The problem of credible commitment is closely related to the so-called "paradox of government." The paradox stipulates that a government that is potentially capable of contributing to the economic performance of society in its protective and productive capacities[17] is, at the same time, equally capable of using its resources to extract wealth from its subjects.

---

[17] The protective capacity of the state consists in the benevolent use of violence for the enforcement of private property and contracts, the productive capacity in the provision of public goods such as defense from foreign and domestic enemies.

The problem with a predatory political environment (even when the community effectively curbs private predation and provides private order) is that it undermines confidence in market activities and limits investment possibilities. Productive entrepreneurship is context-dependent. When the broader legal regime confiscates and extorts from communities in its geographical area, it hinders entrepreneurial activity and innovation.

Arbitrariness by governments creates unstable and insecure economic environments where rational economic actors divert investment into activities that are concealed from the government. Building factories and making long-term investments are less likely to occur when the probability (or magnitude) of government arbitrariness is high, and there is greater uncertainty regarding access to future income when formal sector markets are used. Rational decision-makers take into account expectations concerning future policies before they decide to act. Take for example a country that has a strong past of reneging on promises.

In the context of economic reform and transition, the paradox of government generates the problem of credible commitment. When politicians announce that they will now protect property rights, individuals will be reluctant to start making costly investments at the risk that the government will again defect on its promise, unless it is able to prove to its subjects its credible commitment. According to Boettke (2001), Gorbachev and his government were unable to do so. The combination of a history of predation and insincerity on the part of political leaders, the contradictory nature and deficient implementation of some of the policies contained in the Perestroika plan gave the Russian people elements to believe that Gorbachev was far from resolute and committed to them, thus leading to a result that Boettke summarizes as follows:

> Without conveyance of commitment to market reform, farmers, workers, and others had no incentive to invest in the above-ground market? The Soviet experience shows that without effectively signaling and establishing a binding and credible commitment to broad liberalization, the behavior of the government simply destabilizes the situation.
>
> *(2001, 173)*

3.2   Institutions, Entrepreneurship, and Development

Since the Washington Consensus, ongoing efforts to transport Western institutions of private property rights to former Soviet countries and other transitional economies have been met with failure. Modern Austrians argue that even though property rights are effective, growth-enhancing institutions, they have to emerge from a bottom-up process. Imposing formal institutions into areas that do not have the informal support will not lead to proper adoption and sustainability of those institutions. As we discussed above, Boettke (2001) applies the Austrian framework to understanding the problems of reform in the Soviet Union and how efforts to privatize and create markets from the top-down led to widespread corruption and organized crime. Coyne (2007) finds a similar pattern with importing institutions to the Middle East, where the West's efforts to export democracy to Iraq and Afghanistan failed to stick and exacerbated old problems in those countries. A main result of this literature is that imposing Western institutions on developing or transitional countries without considera-tion of the existing customs and cultural and historical factors will not lead to development and the expected outcomes of the so-called "growth-enhancing" institutions.

Boettke *et al.* (2008: 332) refined understanding of emergent institu-tions by introducing the concept of "institutional stickiness," which is the "ability or inability of new institutional arrangements to take hold where they are transplanted". The stickiness of the institutions depends on how close the institutions are to the norms, customs, and morals, or what is referred to as the metis of society. In this sense, the emergence or bottom-up process of institutional evolution captures this connection to the customs and norms. Thus, institutions that endogenously emerge are more likely to be successful in a particular society, and institutions that are imposed may, or may not, be successful, depending on whether the formal institutions reflect the informal institutions. The implications for this are profound: reform for developing economies has to come from within the country.[18]

The puzzle for institutional economics then becomes one of addressing constraints that different societies may face, which may in turn prevent them from developing the property rights enforcement institutions from the bottom-up. Work in this literature looks to discover how certain cultural traits affect economic performance. How do societies achieve economic growth given cultural constraints? Recent

---

[18] Williamson (2009) provides empirical evidence on the impact of informal institu-tions (that is, institutions that are closer to the metis of a society) on growth.

Austrian-influenced economists have focused on understanding and identifying cultural norms that lead to the development of property rights and better economic performance. Williamson (2011) examines how cultural traits and virtues of trust, individual self-determination, and respect lead to more economic exchange and entrepreneurship by reducing transaction and monitoring costs among the actors and by generating commonalities and focal points. This intuition highlights the idea that when the culture, beliefs, and norms support growth-enhancing institutions, liberal institutions stick and the result is economic development. In other words, "the most sustainable path to progress is an indigenous one" (Boettke 2001: 227).

Further inquiry in this area attempts to identify which conditions lead to thesegrowth-enhancing cultural traits. Work stemming from the Soviet Union shows that politicizing everyday life can hinder the development of important cultural traits. These problems were prevalent in the Soviet Union and are attributed to how the regime bred a parasitic mentality, causing the loss of individual responsibility and destroying civil society (Sobchak, 1991). This is a fruitful area of research for both Austrian and institutional economists, and this work also complements broader mainstream research in economics and culture. A crucial question is: what conditions can facilitate the development of growth-enhancing cultural traits (such as trust, individual self-determination, individual respect) instead of suppressing them (as socialist institutions have done)? Lesson (2005) has set-forth an interesting path in this inquiry by identifying how heterogeneous groups were able to find ways to signal trust to each other in pre-colonial Africa. The implication of Leeson's research is that without nation-states, which often suppress important growth-enhancing traits, individuals were able to find ways to develop trust. Scholars Gellar (2005) and Sawyer (2005) also provide some insights when they discuss how the decline and collapse of states in parts of Africa led to the creation of autonomous self-governing communities and voluntary associations where the individuals developed (or continued to use) their own internal governance rules and mechanisms for sanctioning members.

While the Austrians' early contributions were about identifying how private property rights are necessary for development and growth, modern Austrians have extended Hayek's original insights in the area of spontaneous and emergent orders and used the framework to understand how these institutions of private property can emerge, and to what extent they are influenced by cultural and historical conditions. Austrian insights on the importance of bottom-up institutions has shed light on decades of failures to transport and impose liberal-style Western institutions in countries where these institutions did not arise from the bottom-up.

In exploring the importance of institutions, Austrian scholars have also placed emphasis on the role of the entrepreneur. Analysis of entrepreneurial activity became one of their key contributions, because the extent of entrepreneurial activity depends on the institutions that govern it. Israel Kirzner, a student of Mises, introduced a "pure theory" of entrepreneurship which attempted to provide an explanation of the equilibrating tendency of the market process, the so-called "law of one price" (1973). In Kirzner's theory, sheer ignorance is a pervasive feature of any market. This ignorance leads to violations of the law of one price, that is to say, there exists price differentials for the same good that are not justifiable in terms of transportation or transaction costs. At the same time, these price differentials can be exploited by "alert" individuals who can make pure economic profit by buying low and selling high. Although at any given moment in time sheer ignorance is still present, the entrepreneurial market process "works" towards its reduction, thus leading the market toward (a never truly reachable) equilibrium.

Institutions as the "rules of the game" of society can alter the incentives and payoffs of those engaging in Kirznerian-type entrepreneurship. Boettke and Coyne (2009) have exploited this intellectual connection between entrepreneurship and institutions by discussing how the institutional-setting can influence the type of entrepreneurial activity that economic actors engage in, and also how institutions influence social, political, or institutional entrepreneurs.

Only under a certain institutional environment will entrepreneurs have an incentive to discover new resources, substitutes for existing resources or trading partners to obtain resources, only in certain institutional contexts will entrepreneurs have an incentive to discover new technological knowledge such as new production processes or new organization structures. *(Boettke and Coyne 2009, 158)*

Baumol (1990) was one of the first to make the distinction between productive, unproductive, and destructive entrepreneurship, where the former is the embodiment of the Kirznerian entrepreneur who finds it profitable to engage in such activities as arbitrage and innovation. These activities are productive because, as the entrepreneur discovers previously unexploited opportunities, s/he channels resources to their most highly valued uses (the efficient production point on PPF) and also innovates and finds better ways of producing (shifts the PPF outward). Holcombe (1998) also describes how productive entrepreneurial activity contributes to the development of new markets and thus new productive entrepreneurial opportunities. In this way, productive entrepreneurship creates and builds new productive opportunities, which creates more productive opportunities, and this spurs future growth.

Unproductive entrepreneurial activities include rent-seeking and the political redistribution of resources (Tullock 1967). When there is relatively greater benefit to engaging in unproductive activities, entrepreneurs will spend more resources on rent-seeking and lobbying to redistribute wealth from individuals to the entrepreneur. Destructive entrepreneurship reduces overall wealth in an effort to reallocate wealth that involves destroying existing resources. Institutions can shape the relative payoffs from partaking in productive, unproductive, or destructive entrepreneurial activities. For example, poor protection of property rights makes it less profitable to engage in business ventures, or if the tax system is set-up in such a way that punishes business profits, entrepreneurs will divert their resources into other more profitable ventures. Hence, if the "rules of the game" are such that lobbying efforts yield more reward than exploiting arbitrage opportunities, entrepreneurial activities will be unproductive and destructive, thereby preventing economic development or creating economic decline.

Coyne *et al.* (2010) describe how unproductive entrepreneurial activities breed more unproductive opportunities by creating unproductive niches for profit, altering the pattern of incentives in that society, and creating unproductive social capital and networks. Through these mechanisms, unproductive entrepreneurship breeds more unproductive opportunities for entrepreneurs to exploit, which further minimizes productive activity and growth. Understanding the importance of entrepreneurial activity for economic development is an important first step, but when connecting Austrian insights with institutional economics, we can see that different political institutional arrangements can support or encourage this productive economic activity. Hence, it is important to consider political constraints, and how weak or absent the constraints are helps us to determine the extent of unproductive entrepreneurship and the threat it poses for economic growth.

Institutions can also influence social and political entrepreneurship. Social entrepreneurial activity is often referred to as a non-profit or an independent sector activity. Chamlee-Wright and Storr (2008; 2010) and Storr and Haeffele-Balch (2012) have documented remarkable examples of successful social entrepreneurship and community-based activities where the states and markets have failed, such as helping the needy, providing solutions to natural disasters, and solving various collective action problems. Just as institutions influence entrepreneurial market activities, they also alter the costs and benefits of engaging in social entrepreneurship and community-based solutions to collective action problems. Elinor Ostrom (1998; 2005) has explored how the political structures can influence the extent to which communities can create their own rules to overcome "tragedy of the commons" problems and co-produce such things as public safety. The mechanisms through which civil societies and community solutions are able to foster their successes is through their ability to utilize local knowledge and their avoidance of many public choice problems that can plague governments at larger levels.

Similarly, institutions can influence political entrepreneurs when political institutions create different profit opportunities. There are two levels of political entrepreneurship: the first level is that of ordinary politics where the entrepreneurs can gain from legislative activity within the given political structure. In this sense, the entrepreneurs are those individuals who are alert and act upon opportunities that exist in government. This can be done through catering to special interest groups to further their agendas. The second level of entrepreneurship refers to exploiting opportunities in the actual structure of government. On the first level, the political entrepreneur takes the structure as given and exploits opportunities within the structure.

On the second level, the entrepreneur (referred to as the institutional entrepreneur) is involved in changing the fundamental constitution and rules of the game. Coyne and Leeson (2009) examine the media's role for institutional entrepreneurial activities and conclude that the media is one mechanism for facilitating productive institutional entrepreneurship.

Changing the institutional structures to encourage productive entrepreneurship is "productive political entrepreneurship," while altering the rules of the game so that it breeds more unproductive entrepreneurship is called "unproductive political entrepreneurship." Boettke and Leeson (2008) analyze how institutional entrepreneurs were able to create rules to foster cooperation where formal governments were absent in Somalia. Unlike entrepreneurship in the market, political and social entrepreneurs have no rational economic calculation with which to ensure a tendency toward the allocation of resources to their most highly valued uses, since there is nothing that plays a similar role to property, prices, and profits/losses as in market settings.

3.3   Spontaneous Orders, Self-Enforcing Exchanges, and Self-Governance

The economics and political economy of anarchic institutional arrangements have been quickly growing areas of research on how individuals are able to supply justice systems, law enforcement, and create order without the need of a central authority. Modern Austrians are studying the presence and robustness of spontaneous orders and are advancing our empirical understanding of how far the frontiers of self-governance can be extended (Leeson 2008c).

One way of revealing spontaneous order mechanisms is showing how groups of individuals, though they may be under a government, choose not to rely on the services provided by the government and find their own mechanisms of providing law and order. These cases are "in the shadow of the state" because the order that is provided is within the purview of the state. In situations where government services are too costly or ineffective, individuals often choose to create their own systems of governance. Self-governance institutions rely on a variety of mechanisms.

Reputation is a frequently studied mechanism that promotes social order. For example, consider a simple market transaction between a buyer and seller. If the buyer paid for two soft pretzels but the seller only gave him one soft pretzel, the buyer could sue the seller for not upholding his end of the contract. However, the costs of using the legal system are higher than the benefits the buyer would get from a successful verdict in his favor. Does this mean that sellers can always get away with cheating the buyers on small transactions? Anecdotally, we know this is not the case, as sellers will often go out of their way to satisfy the consumers, and they sometimes apply the motto that "the customer is always right."

The reason sellers do not cheat the buyers in small transactions is because the reputation of the seller acts as a mechanism for safeguarding against contractual opportunism. When sellers cheat buyers, buyers can boycott the store and spread the word to other buyers. Hence, reputations are mechanisms of contractual enforcement whereby parties that can engage in opportunism will have an incentive not to do so, because it will ruin their reputation and reduce future income. This type of mechanism is "self-enforcing" since parties to the agreement have an incentive to enforce and abide by the agreement, and this is crucial to understanding the effectiveness of self-governing communities. A powerful example of self-governance and self-enforcing contracts in "the shadow of the state" is how Jewish diamond traders in New York City use reputation mechanisms to govern diamond trading and facilitate cooperation in this industry. As Bernstein (1992) and Richman (2006) discuss, diamond traders have access to the state court and governance system, but choose to rely instead on their own internal governance system, as it is better able to enforce contractual agreements and thereby facilitate commerce in their industry.

Stringham (2002, 2003, 2015) explores the role of private governance institutions in the origins and development of the stock market in Amsterdam and London in the seventeenth and eighteenth centuries. These experiences are illustrative of the ability of economic agents to come up with solutions to the problem of governance in the absence of state enforcement. In 1610, the Dutch government introduced a law against the exchange of financial instruments, as these were associated more with gambling than with productive economic activities (Stringham 2015: 39). Notwithstanding the actions of the government, futures and short sales became very popular in the Amsterdam stock market. Although they could not rely on public courts for the enforcement of financial contracts involving the outlawed instruments, brokers kept dealing in them quite successfully. This was made possible by the discipline of continuous dealing that emerged among brokers. Reputation played a fundamental role in making this system work: "Despite the fact that anyone could enter the Bourse, traders had to build their reputations before they could make substantial trades" (Stringham 2015: 57). Not only was the Dutch stock exchange sustainable in the absence of state enforcement – or, to be more precise, in the presence of state hostility towards it – but it was a very dynamic and innovative one, and was able to support large and complex transactions.

The English experience was somewhat parallel to that of the Netherlands. The English parliament outlawed the formation of new joint stock companies in 1720 and banned a variety of financial instruments in 1734. Although the latter were "all but unenforceable . . . stockbrokers engaged in them anyway" (Stringham 2015: 67). Unlike their Dutch predecessors, English brokers did not just rely on continuous dealing to discipline exchange in the financial market. Instead, they used a local coffeehouse – the Jonathan's – as their base. People who failed to keep their word were expelled from the Jonathan's and their names written on its walls, thus reducing their ability to interact with other traders.

Eventually, traders founded a coffeehouse of their own – the New Jonathan – and established a private club with a written constitution and well-specified rules, the purpose of which was a reduction of transaction costs – including the cost associated with the possibility of cheating – among its members. Cheaters were punished by the club through its rule-enforcement agency: the Committee for General Purposes. Penalties could go from the payment of a fine and the compensation of the other party to temporary and even permanent expulsion. The effectiveness of these private governance institutions is attested to by the success of the New Jonathan, which eventually became the London Stock-Exchange (Stringham 2015: 74–75).

Leeson (2007a, 2009) studies how seventeenth and eighteenth century pirates created their own complex constitutions and rules that governed their behavior. The rules they created were specific to the problems that they faced. For example, pirates often relied on regulations against smoking and drinking instead of creating property rights to address these negative externalities. The conditions onboard were such that the transaction costs of pirate negotiations to compensate for the right to smoke were sufficiently higher than just having a rule that prohibited or restricted smoking to certain areas of the ship (Leeson 2009: 70–71). Pirates also formed elaborate constitutions that included checks on the abuses of the pirate captain by creating such clauses as the separation of power.

Pirates were outlaws and therefore serve as a striking example of governance that emerged in the absence of state law. Leeson (2010: 143) explains, "[g]overnment did not enforce employment agreements between pirates or other piratical contracts, nor did it prevent or punish theft or violence between pirates, and so on. Pirates existed in a state of utter anarchy." Similarly, Anderson and Hill (2004) provide an important study of the spontaneous orders that emerged outside of the existence of state law. They describe the American West as being in a state of anarchy between 1830 and 1900 since there was no formal government that provided law and order to Americans migrating to the west. Communities instead formed associations to provide public goods and rules that governed acquiring unowned land. These examples directly tie-in to the research agenda of Austrian economists who are interested in understanding how coordination is achieved, and they rely on Hayek's emphasis of the importance of decentralized rule-making.

Skarbek (2011) analyzes the *Mexican Mafia* in California and demonstrates the system of governance that emerged to facilitate trade by Hispanic drug dealers in Los Angeles. Skarbek (2010) also examines the governance structure of the *La Nuestra Familia* prison gang in California and how it evolved to solve the collective action problems that are connected with multilevel criminal enterprises. These rules emerge as private individuals devise mechanisms to solve their dilemmas and to find ways to promote social cooperation in order to realize mutually beneficial exchange with each other.

Skarbek's work (2014, see also Skarbek 2012, 2016), shows how an exogenous shock – in this case, the sudden increase in the inmate population since the 1980s – can foster spontaneous institutional evolution. Before the shock, social order within prisons was guaranteed by the "convict code," a set of customary norms that relied mostly on ostracism as a system of decentralized enforcement. This system was made ineffective by the increase in social, cultural, and ethnic heterogeneity of the American penal system. Initially, the fall of the "convict code" resulted in an increase in violence, but eventually led to the rise of prison gangs. Prison gangs worked as stationary bandits in a context in which the formal authorities (i.e. the penal system itself) was both unable and unwilling to provide inmates with a decent level of personal safety, the protection of property rights, and the enforcement of contracts.

Another characteristic of emergent and private governance institutions is that they engender an important aspect of legitimacy, which is often lacking in situations where rules are imposed. Community members are more likely to violate rules if they perceive them as illegitimate, which Elinor Ostrom notes is often the case when these rules are imposed on the community from the outside (Ostrom 1990). When rules are seen as legitimate, this lowers the enforcement and monitoring costs of the rules (Ostrom 1990: 205). Further, Ostrom finds that when citizens create their own rules, they can design them in such a way to minimize monitoring and enforcement costs. She notes that depending on the arrangement of rules, monitoring can be a "natural by-product" (Ostrom 1990: 96).

Ostrom illustrates that citizens use knowledge from experience to create enforceable rules with potentially embedded monitoring costs, thereby helping to ensure the effectiveness of these rules. Furthermore, the problem of regulations that come from the top-down is that they are often ineffective and counterproductive because they do not know the specific conditions and problems that govern these communities. These rules emerge because there are gains to be made from cooperation and exchange and thus individuals have an incentive to create constitutions and rules to govern behavior and to mitigate the problems of negative externalities or disputes that threaten the achievement of their goals.

Lastly, the study of private governance is an exercise in understanding self-enforcing contract mechanisms, since the decision to join or leave the group is voluntary. Potentially unhappy pirates can leave a pirate ship if they believe that they have been "cheated." If captains abuse their powers and break the constitutional contract that has been set-up between all the crewmembers, pirates may join other ships and this in turn reduces the revenue of the captain and that pirate ship. In other words, private governance systems create an incentive to abide by contractual agreements in a competitive environment, thus making these rules self-enforcing.

A broader area that has garnered Austrian attention is international law. International law was not imposed by any one country, but rather emerged as a mechanism for taking advantage of international trade (Leeson 2008b). Private courts, such as the International Chamber of Commerce (ICC) International Court of Arbitration, exist to facilitate trade among merchants from all over the world. In their trade agreements, merchants will specify one of the many private arbitration companies to handle their disputes. Unlike governments that can enforce decisions formally, reputational mechanisms also govern many of these trades. Thus, even without a formal force backing contractual agreements, international buyers and sellers voluntarily comply with the private arbitration court's decisions. Historically, modern international trade governance institutions evolved out of the medieval trading customs, which eventually evolved into a body of private international law called the "law merchant" (Benson 1989). Additionally, Austrians have attempted to evaluate the effectiveness of these emergent institutions in facilitating cooperation relative to the more top-down approaches. Leeson (2007b) and Powell *et al.* (2008), for example, have both analyzed the performance of Somalia under anarchy relative to how it performed under a government. Performance indicators show that even though the conditions in Somalia are not ideal, they have improved welfare relative to when the country had a dictatorial government. In this sense, Austrians are engaging debates on comparative political institutions by analyzing how the performance of different political regimes (anarchy vs. dictatorial government) impact economic performance.

The economics of superstition and the role it plays in ensuring the effectiveness of self-governance institutions has been a recent development in the economic analysis of institutions by contemporary Austrian economists (Leeson 2012; Leeson and Suarez 2015). The economics of superstition offers insights into the relationship between two classic themes in Austrian economics: subjectivism (with special reference to scientifically incorrect beliefs) and spontaneous order. Historically, many societies and groups could not rely on formal governance institutions for the provision of adjudication, the enforcement of property rights, and the solution of collective action problems. In those instances in which private and public solutions to these problems were outside the opportunity set of society, superstition often provided a workable, spontaneously emerged alternative.

Leeson and Coyne (2012) study the traditional Liberian adjudication institution known as Sassywood.[19] In case of litigation, this institution required the defendant to swallow a poisonous liquid. In case of innocence, all-knowing magic spirits would help the defendant by making him vomit the poison. If guilty, the spirits would do nothing and the defendant would instead be killed by the ingestion. The effectiveness of this institution rests on the fact that the members of this society believed in the existence of spirits, and that these spirits would behave the way described above. The fear of getting killed by the poison will push the guilty defendant to admit guilt, while the innocent one, free of fear, will drink. Thus, this institution is self-enforcing, and, because the beliefs upon which it relies are unfalsifiable, it is also self-perpetuating.

Leeson (2013) provides an economic analysis of Romaniya, the customary system of norm of the Vlax Roma Gypsies. Some Gypsie communities live in self-imposed isolation from the rest of society and cannot therefore rely on the governments of their countries for the enforcement of the Romaniya. Thus, these communities developed a set of superstitions based on the twin notions of marime (ritual pollution) and vujo (ritual purity). Failing to abide to the rules of Romanyia results in marime. This condition of ritual pollution is contagious, which ensures that those who violate the law are effectively ostracized. In the absence of government, and without the superstitious beliefs in purity and pollution, Romanyia will be ineffective. Once again, superstition enables social cooperation in an anarchic situation.

Leeson (2014b) provides another case study, this time focused on the role of superstition in sustaining the enforcement of property rights in the absence of effective governments. Religious communities in tenth century western France could not rely on public courts and police forces for protection. In order to enforce their property rights, communities of monks resorted to liturgical maledictions. The three most popular forms of malediction were maledictio proper (prayers used to damn an individual or group of individuals that were found guilty of some crime against the religious community), clamors (the appeal to God for the punishment of those that had disrespected God's servants), and, finally, the most extreme of the three – excommunication. To be excommunicated means being ostracized from the Christian faith, but in a context in

---

[19] Leeson (2014a) provides a rational choice explanation of another African institution for the adjudication of disputes, the menge oracle used by the Azande.

which almost every member of society shares a belief in the Christian faith, the existence of God, paradise, and hell, it also practically resulted in ostracism from the secular community as well. Given the existence of these underlying religious beliefs, malediction worked as an effective enforcement mechanism for communities of monks in medieval Europe.

4 Conclusion

The message from Austrian and institutional economics comes in three main parts. First, markets are the key to development and economic growth. Second, for markets to operate effectively, they require governance institutions that protect property rights from both private and public predation, settle disputes, and foster an environment that allows for social cooperation, exchange, and productive entrepreneurship. Third, effective governance structures arise from the bottom-up as individuals seek to take advantage of mutually beneficial exchanges, and these structures are successful because they are embedded in the local knowledge, underlying norms of the society, and have self-enforcing properties. Given these main implications, there are still great limitations to understanding how the path to growth can be achieved.

Are emergent orders always beneficial? Insights from both Austrian and institutional economics can answer this question in different ways. We have discussed the success of emergent rules and institutions as they take into account the local knowledge, underlying customs, and norms of the communities, and are self-enforcing. But Martin and Storr (2008) discuss how emergent orders that are ingrained in negative belief systems or mob behavior actually fail to lead to social cooperation and mutually beneficial exchange and instead lead to more conflict. Is this a function of emergent-order properties underperforming or is it a function of the underlying constraints that such communities face? Would a top-down approach be better able to foster cooperation in this type of community? These are important questions to examine, and it is essential to consider that negative belief systems are a constraint on society and the type of institutions that can develop. In this sense, the emergent-order would be seen as the "best they can do," given the cultural traits. But as we noted above, there is evidence that certain conditions can change cultural traits overtime, and it is important to understand how the political structure can lead to the development of cultural traits. Change in political structure can come from the role of the institutional entrepreneur in taking the initiative to change governance structures, for better or for worse.

Furthermore, the effectiveness of rules depends on how well they cater to the specific needs and goals of the communities. The vast diversity of individuals in unique social, religious, or ethnic groups speaks to the limitations in creating top-down rules over a broad range of heterogeneous communities. There is no "one-size-fits-all" institutional regime. In fact, the heterogeneity of communities implies that perhaps governments should be organized more like private groups or clubs. The political structure of polycentricism in this case may be able to meet the needs and desires of diverse communities who can engage in constitutional making from the bottom-up. When structures of government consolidate and attempt to impose one-size-fit-all rules in the face of sharp heterogeneous communities, it will be confronted with extremely high enforcement costs which could undermine already existing social norms, thereby causing conflict.

At some level, scholars researching in Austrian and institutional economics have to embrace that various constraints limit development and growth, and that there is not much that outsiders can do except to allow freedom of entry and exit for competition between communities and movement among individuals. While the work in Austrian and institutional economics have brought us far, there is still much research to be done in this area if we are to understandthe important factors that lead to development, as well as the constraints, and the processes by which institutions can evolve and change over time,.

References

1. Acemoglu, Daron, Simon Johnson, and James A. Robinson. 2001 "The Colonial Origins of Comparative Development: An Empirical Investigation." *American Economic Review* 91(5): 1369–1401.
2. Alchian, Armen. 1965. "Some Economics of Property Rights." *Il Politico*: 816–829.
3. Alchian, Armen and Arold Demsetz. 1973. "The Property Rights Paradigm." *The Journal of Economic History* 33(1): 16–27.
4. Aligica, Paul D. 2013. *Institutional Diversity and Political Economy: The Ostroms and Beyond*. New York: Oxford University Press.

5. Aligica, Paul D. and Peter J. Boettke. 2009. *Challenging Institutional Analysis and Development: The Bloomington School*. New York: Routledge.
6. Anderson, Terry and P.J. Hill. 2004. *The Not So Wild, Wild West*. Stanford, CA: Stanford University Press.
7. Barzel, Yoram. 1997. *Economic Analysis of Property Rights*. Cambridge: Cambridge University Press.
8. Baumol, William. 1990. "Entrepreneurship: Productive, Unproductive, and Destructive." *Journal of Political Economy* 98(5): 893–921.
9. Beaulier, Scott. 2008. "Look, Botswana: No Hands! Why Botswana's Government Should Let the Economy Steer Itself." In Benjamin Powell (ed.) *Making Poor Nations Rich*. Stanford, CA: Stanford University Press.
10. Benson, Bruce L. 1989. "Spontaneous Evolution of Commercial Law." *Southern Economic Journal* 55(3): 644–661.
11. Bernstein, Lisa. 1992. "Opting Out the Legal System." *The Journal of Legal Studies* 21(1): 115–157.
12. Boettke, Peter J. 1990. *The Political Economy of Soviet Socialism*. Amsterdam: Springer Science.
13. Boettke, Peter J. 1993. *Why Perestroika Failed: The Politics and Economics of Socialist Transformation*. New York: Routledge.
14. Boettke, Peter J. 2000a. "Toward a History of the Theory of Socialist Planning." In Peter J. Boettke (ed.) 2000b. *Socialism and the Market: The Socialist Calculation Debate Revisited*. London: Routledge: 1–39.
15. Boettke, Peter J. (ed.). 2000b. *Socialism and the Market: The Socialist Calculation Debate Revisited*. London: Routledge.
16. Boettke, Peter J. 2001. *Calculation and Coordination: Essays on Socialism and Transitional Political Economy*. London: Routledge.
17. Boettke, Peter J. 2012. *Living Economics*. Oakland: The Independent Institute.
18. Boettke, Peter J. and Rosolino Candela. 2016. "Price Theory as Prophylactic Against Popular Fallacies." George Mason University Working Paper Series No. 16–05.
19. Boettke, Peter J. and Christopher J. Coyne. 2009. "Context Matters: Institutions and Entrepreneurship." *Foundations and Trends in Entrepreneurship* 5(3): 135–209.
20. Boettke, Peter J. and Peter T. Leeson. 2004. "Liberty, Socialism, and Robust Political Economy." *Journal of Markets and Morality* 7(1): 99–111.
21. Boettke, Peter J. and Peter T. Leeson. 2009. "Two-Tiered Entrepreneurship and Economic Development." *International Review of Law and Economics* 29(3): 252–259.

22. Boettke, Peter J., Jayme S. Lemke, and Liya Palagashvili. 2015. "Polycentricity, Self-governance, and the Art & Science of Association." *The Review of Austrian Economics* 28(3): 311–335.

23. Boettke, Peter J. and Kyle W. O'Donnell. 2013. "The Failed Appropriation by F.A. Hayek by Formalist Economics." *Critical Review* 25: 305–341.

24. Boettke, Peter J., Christopher J. Coyne, and Peter T. Leeson. 2008. "Institutional Stickiness and the New Development Economics." *American Journal of Economics and Sociology* 67(2): 331–358.

25. Buchanan, James M. 1987. "The Constitution of Economic Policy." *American Economic Review* 77(3): 243–250.

26. Buchanan, James M. and Gordon Tullock. [1962] 2004. *The Calculus of Consent: The Logical Foudnations of Constitutional Democracy.* Indianapolis: Liberty Fund.

27. Bukharin, Nikolai. 1979. "The Politics and Economics of the Transition Period." Peter J. Boettke (ed.) 2000b. *Socialism and the Market: The Socialist Calculation Debate Revisited.* London: Routledge: 343–472.

28. Caldwell, Bruce. 2004. *Hayek's Challenge: An Intellectual Biography of F.A. Hayek.* Chicago, IL: University of Chicago Press.

29. Chamlee-Wright, Emily and Virgil Storr. 2008. "The Entrepreneur's Role in Post-Disaster Community Recovery: Implications for Post-Disaster Recovery Policy." Mercatus Center Policy Series, Policy Primer No. 6.

30. Chamlee-Wright, Emily and Virgil Storr. 2010. "The Role of Social Entrepreneurship in Post-Disaster Recovery." *International Journal of Innovation and Regional Development* 2(1/2): 149–164.

31. Coase, Ronald H. 1937. "The Nature of the Firm." *Economica* 4(16): 386–405.

32. Coase, Ronald H. 1959. "The Federal Communication Commission." *Journal of Law and Economics* 56(4): 879–915.

33. Coase, Ronald H. 1960. "The Problem of Social Cost." *Journal of Law and Economics* 3: 1–44.

34. Cowan, Robin and Mario J. Rizzo. 1996. "The Genetic-Causal Tradition and Modern Economic Theory." *Kyklos* 49(3): 273–317.

35. Coyne, Christopher J. 2013. *Doing Bad by Doing Good: Why Humanitarian Aid Fails.* Stanford, CA: Stanford University Press.

36. Coyne, Christopher J. 2007. *After War: The Political Economy of Exporting Democracy.* Stanford, CA: Stanford University Press.

37. Coyne, Christopher J. and Peter T. Leeson. 2009. *Media, Development, and Institutional Change.* Cheltenham: Edward Elgar Publishing.

38. Coyne, Christopher J., Russ Sobel, and John Dove. 2010. "The Non-Productive Entrepreneurial Process." *The Review of Austrian Economics* 23(4): 333–346.
39. Crawford, Sue and Elinor Ostrom. 1995. "A Grammar of Institutions." *American Political Science Review* 89(3): 582–600.
40. D'Amico, Daniel J. 2010. "The Prison in Economics: Private and Public Incarceration in Ancient Greece." *Public Choice* 145(3/4): 46–82.
41. Deaton, Angus. 2013. *The Great Escape: Health, Wealth, and the Origins of Inequality.* Princeton, NJ: Princeton University Press.
42. DeCanio, Samuel. 2014. "Democracy, the Market, and the Logic of Social Choice." *American Journal of Political Science* 58(3): 637–652.
43. Demsetz, Harold. 1964. "The Exchange and Enforcement of Property Rights." *Journal of Law and Economics* 7: 11–26.
44. Demsetz, Harold. 1966. "Some Aspects of Property Rights." *Journal of Law and Economics* 9: 61–70.
45. Demsetz, Harold. 1967. "Toward a Theory of Property Rights." *American Economic Review* 57(2): 347–359.
46. Djankov, Simeon, Rafael La Porta, Florencio Lopez-de-Silanes, and Andrei Shleifer. 2003. "Courts: The Lex Mundi Project." *The Quarterly Journal of Economics* (118): 453–517.
47. Ferguson, Adam. [1767] 1995. *An Essay on the History of Civil Society.* Cambridge: Cambridge University Press.
48. Gellar, Sheldon. 2005. *Democracy in Senegal.* New York: Palgrave.
49. Glaeser, Edward L. and Andrei Shleifer. 2002. "Legal Origins." *Quarterly Journal of Economics* 117(4): 1193–1229.
50. Hayek, Friedrich A. 1937. "Economics and Knowledge." *Economica* 4(13): 33–54.
51. Hayek, Friedrich A. 1940. "The Socialist Calculation: The Competitive Solution." *Economica* 7(26): 125–149.
52. Hayek, Friedrich A. [1944] 2007. *The Road to Serfdom.* Chicago, IL: University of Chicago Press.
53. Hayek, Friedrich A. 1945. "The Use of Knowledge in Society." *American Economic Review* 35(4): 519–530.
54. Hayek, Friedrich A. 1946. "The Meaning of Competition." In Friedrich A. Hayek. 1948. *Individualism and Economic Order.* Chicago, IL: University of Chicago Press: 92–106.
55. Hayek, Friedrich A. 1948. *Individualism and Economic Order.* Chicago, IL: University of Chicago Press.
56. Hayek, Friedrich A. [1952a] 1980. *The Counterrevolution of Science: Studies on the Use and Abuse of Reason.* Indianapolis: Liberty Press.

57. Hayek, Friedrich A. [1952b] 1972. *The Sensory Order: An Inquiry Into the Foundations of Theoretical Psychology.* Chicago, IL: University of Chicago Press.

58. Hayek, Friedrich A. [1960] 1978. *The Constitution of Liberty.* Chicago, IL: University of Chicago Press.

59. Hayek, Friedrich A. [1961] 2014. "A New Look at Economic Theory." In Bruce Caldwell (ed.). *The Market and Other Orders.* Chicago: Chicago University Press: 373–426.

60. Hayek, F.A. 1973. *Law, Legislation and Liberty: Rules and Order,* Volume 1. Chicago: University of Chicago Press.

61. Hayek, F.A. 1988. *The Fatal Conceit: The Errors of Socialism.* Chicago, IL: University of Chicago Press.

62. Holcombe, Randall. 1998. "Entrepreneurship and economic growth." *The Quarterly Journal of Austrian Economics* 1(2): 45–62.

63. Kirzner, Israel M. 1973. *Competition and Entrepreneurship.* Chicago, IL: University of Chicago Press.

64. Kirzner, Israel M. 1988. "The Socialist Calculation Debate: Lessons for Austrians." *Review of Austrian Economics* 2(1): 1–18.

65. Klein, Peter G. 1999. "New Institutional Economics." *Encyclopedia of Law and Economics.* Cheltenham: Edward Elgar: 456–489.

66. Knight, Frank H. 1936. "The Place of Marginal Economics in a Collectivist System." *American Economic Review* 26(1): 255–266.

67. Lange, Oskar. 1936–7. "On the Economic Theory of Socialism." *The Review of Economic Studies* 4: 53–71 and 123–142.

68. La Porta, Rafael, Florencio Lopez-de-Silanes, Andrei Shleifer, and Robert Vishny. 1998. "Law and Finance." *Journal of Political Economy* 106: 1113–1155.

69. Lavoie, Don. [1985] 2015. *Rivalry and Central Planning: The Socialist Calculation Debate Reconsidered.* Arlington: Mercatus Center.

70. Leeson, Peter T. 2005. "Endogenizing Fractionalization." *Journal of Institutional Economics* 1(1): 75–98.

71. Leeson, Peter T. 2007. "An-arrgh-chy: The Law and Economics of Pirate Organization." *Journal of Political Economy* 115(6): 1049–1094.

72. Leeson, Peter T. 2007b. "Better off Stateless: Somalia Before and After Government Collapse." *Journal of Comparative Economics* 35(4): 689–710.

73. Leeson, Peter T. 2008. "Social Distance and Self-enforcing Exchange." *Journal of Legal Studies* 37(1): 161–188.

74. Leeson, Peter T. 2008b. "How Important is State Enforcement in Trade?" *American Law and Economic Review* 10(1): 61–89.

75. Leeson, Peter T. 2008c. "Coordination Without Command." *Public Choice* 135(1–2): 67–78.

76. Leeson, Peter T. 2009. *The Invisible Hook: The Hidden Economics of Pirates.* Princeton, NJ: Princeton University Press.
77. Leeson, Peter T. 2010. "How Much Order Can Spontaneous Order Create?" in Peter Boettke (ed.) 2000b. *Handbook on Contemporary Austrian Economics.* Cheltenham, Edward Elgar Publishing.
78. Leeson, Peter T. 2012. "An Austrian Approach to Law and Economics with Special Reference to Superstition." *Review of Austrian Economics* 25(3): 185–198.
79. Leeson, Peter T. 2013. "Gypsy Law." *Public Choice* 155(3–4): 273–292.
80. Leeson, Peter T. 2014a. "Oracles." *Rationality and Society* 26(2): 141–169.
81. Leeson, Peter T. 2014b. "God Damn." *Journal of Law, Economics, and Organization* 30(1): 193–216.
82. Leeson, Peter T. and Christopher J. Coyne. 2012. "Sassywood." *Journal of Comparative Economics* 40(4): 608–620.
83. Leeson, Peter T. and Paola Suarez. 2015. "Superstition and Self-Governance." *Advances in Austrian Economics* 19: 47–66.
84. Lenin, Vladimir I. 1920. "The State and Revolution." In Peter J. Boettke (ed.) 2000b. *Socialism and the Market: The Socialist Calculation Debate Revisited.* London: Routledge: 213–339.
85. Lerner, Abba P. 1934–5. "Economic Theory and Socialist Economy." *The Review of Economic Studies* 2: 51–61.
86. Lerner, Abba P. 1937. "Statics and Dynamics in Socialist Economics." *The Economic Journal* 47(186): 253–270.
87. Mahoney, Paul G. 2001. "The Common Law and Economic Growth: Hayek Might Be Right." *Journal of Legal Studies* 30:503–525.
88. Martin, Nona and Virgil Storr. 2008. "On Perverse Emergent Orders." *Studies in Emergent Orders* 1: 73–91.
89. Marx, Karl. 1938. "Critique of the Gotha Programme." In Peter J. Boettke (ed.) 2000b. *Socialism and the Market: The Socialist Calculation Debate Revisited.* London: Routledge: 41–75.
90. Medema, Steven G. and Richard O. Zerbe Jr. 1999. "The Coase Theorem." *Encyclopedia of Law and Economics.* Cheltenham: Edward Elgar: 836–892.
91. Menger, Carl. [1871] 2007. *Principles of Economics.* Auburn: The Ludwig von Mises Institute.
92. Menger, Carl. [1882] 2009. *Investigations into the Methods of the Social Sciences with Special Reference to Economics.* Auburn: The Ludwig von Mises Institute.
93. Mises, Ludwig von. [1920] 1990. *Economic Calculation in the Socialist Commonwealth.* Auburn: The Ludwig von Mises Institute.
94. Mises, Ludwig von. [1922] 1981. *Socialism: An Economic and Sociological Analysis.* Indianapolis: Liberty Press.

95. Mises, Ludwig von. [1933] 2003. *Epistemological Problems of Economics*. Auburn: The Ludwig von Mises Institute.
96. North, Douglass C. 1981. *Structure and Change in Economic History*. New York: Norton.
97. North, Douglass C. 1990. *Institutions, Institutional Change, and Economic Performance*. Cambridge: Cambridge University Press.
98. North, Douglass C. 2005. *Understanding the Process of Economic Change*. Cambridge: Cambridge University Press.
99. North, Douglass C., John J. Wallis, and Barry R. Weingast. 2009. *Violence and Social Orders: A Conceptual Framework for Interpreting Recorded Human History*. Cambridge: Cambridge University Press.
100. Olson, Mancur. [1965] 2002. *The Logic of Collective Action*. Cambridge, MA: Harvard University Press.
101. Olson, Mancur. 1993. "Dictatorship, Democracy, and Development." *American Political Science Review* 87(3): 567–576.
102. Ostrom, Elinor. 1990. *Governing the Commons: The Evolution of Institutions for Collective Action*. Cambridge: Cambridge University Press.
103. Ostrom, Elinor. 1998. "The Comparative Study of Public Economies." *The American Economist*, 42(1): 3–17
104. Ostrom, Elinor. 2005. "Policies that Crowd out Reciprocity and Collective Action." In Herbert Gintis, Samuel Bowles, Robert Boyd, and Ernst Fehr, *Moral Sentiments and Material Interests: The Foundations of Cooperation in Economic Life*. Cambridge, MA: MIT Press: 253–275.
105. Ostrom, Elinor. 2010. "Beyond Markets and States: Polycentric Governance of Complex Economic Systems." *American Economic Review* 100: 641–672.
106. Ostrom, Elinor and Hess, Charlotte. 2008. "Private and Common Property Rights." *Encyclopedia of Law and Economics*. Northampton: Edward Elgar.
107. Ostrom, E. and G. Whitaker. 1973. "Does Local Community Control of Police Make a Difference?" *American Journal of Political Science* 17(1): 48–76. Reprinted in Michael McGinnis (ed.) *Polycentricity and Local Public Economies*. Ann Arbor, MI: University of Michigan Press, 1999.
108. Ostrom, Vincent. 1980. "Artisanship and Artifact." *Public Administration Review* 40(4): 309–317.
109. Ostrom, Vincent. 1999. "Polycentricity." In Michael D. McGinnis (ed.) *Polycentricity and Local Public Economies*. Ann Arbor, MI: University of Michigan Press.
110. Parks, Roger and Ronald Oakerson. 1988. Metropolitan Organization: The St. Louis Case. United States Advisory Commission on Intergovernmental Relations Report M-158. Washington, DC.

111. Pennington, Mark. 2011. "Robust Political Economy." *Policy: A Journal of Public Policy and Ideas* 27(4): 8.

112. Powell, Benjamin, Ryan Ford, and Alex Nowrasteh. 2008. "Somalia after State Collapse: Chaos or Improvement?" *Journal of Economic Behavior and Organization* 67: 657–670.

113. Powell, Benjamin and Edward Stringham. 2009. "Public Choice and the Economic Analysis of Anarchy: A Survey." *Public Choice* 140 (3/4): 503–538.

114. Prychitko, David. 2008. "Marxism." In, David H. Henderson (ed.) *Concise Encyclopedia of Economics*. Indianapolis: Liberty Fund.

115. Richman, Barak. 2006. "How Community Institutions Create Economic Advantage: Jewish Diamond Merchants in New York." *Law and Social Inquiry* 31(2): 383–420.

116. Rizzo, Mario. 1999. "Which Kind of Legal Order? Logical Coherence and Praxeological Coherence." *Journal des Economistes et des Etudes Humaines* 9(4): 497–510.

117. Rodrik, Dani, Arvind Subrmanian, and Francesco Trebbi. 2004. "Institutions Rule: The Primacy of Institutions Over Geography and Integration in Economic Development." *Journal of Economic Growth* 9(2): 131–165.

118. Sawyer, Amos. 2005. *Beyond Plunder: Toward Democratic Governance in Liberia*. Boulder, CO: Lynne Rienner Publisher.

119. Schumpeter, Joseph A. [1942] 2008. *Capitalism, Socialism, and Democracy*. London: Routledge.

120. Skarbek, David. 2010. "Putting the 'Con' into Constitutions: The Economics of Prison Gangs." *Journal of Law Economics and Organization* 26(2): 183–211.

121. Skarbek, David. 2011. "Governance and Prison Gangs." *American Political Science Review* 105(4): 702–716.

122. Skarbek, David. 2012. "Prison Gangs, Norms, and Organizations." *Journal of Economic Behavior & Organization* 82(1): 96–109.

123. Skarbek, David. 2014. *The Social Order of the Underworld: How Prison Gangs Govern the American Penal System*. Oxford: Oxford University Press.

124. Skarbek, David. 2016. "Covenants without the Sword? Comparing Prison Self-Governance Globally." *American Political Science Review* 110(4): 845–862.

125. Sobchak, Anatoly. 1991. "Transition to a Market Economy." *Cato Journal* 11(2): 195–205.

126. Stigler, George. 1992. "Law or Economics?" *Journal of Law and Economics* 35(2): 455–468.

127. Storr, Virgil and Stephanie Haeffele-Balch. 2012. "Post Disaster Community Recovery in Heterogeneous Loosely-Connected Communities." *Review of Social Economy* 70(3): 295–314.
128. Stringham, Edward P. 2002. "The Emergence of the London Stock-Exchange as Self-Policing Club." *Journal of Private Enterprise* 17(2): 1–19.
129. Stringham, Edward P. 2003. "The Extralegal Development of Securities Trading in Seventeenth Century Amsterdam." *The Quarterly Review of Economics and Finance.* 43(2): 321–344.
130. Stringham, Edward P. 2015. *Private Governance: Creating Order in Economic and Social Life.* Oxford: Oxford University Press.
131. Tabellini, Guido. 2010. "Culture and Institutions: Economic Development in the Regions of Europe." *Journal of the European Economic Association* 8(4): 677–716.
132. Tullock, Gordon. 1967. "The Welfare Costs of Tariffs, Monopolies, and Theft." *Economic Inquiry* 5(3), 224–232.
133. Tullock, Gordon. 1974. *The Social Dilemma: The Economics of War and Revolution.*Blacksburg: University Publications.
134. Williamson, Claudia R. 2009. "Informal Institutions Rule: Institutional Arrangements and Economic Performance." *Public Choice* 139(3–4): 371–387.
135. Williamson, Claudia R. 2011. "Civilizing Society." *The Journal of Private Enterprise* 27: 99–120.
136. Williamson, Oliver E. 2002. "The New Institutional Economics: Taking Stocks, Looking Ahead." *Journal of Economic Literature* 38(3): 595–613.
137. Zywicki, Todd. 2008. "Spontaneous Order and the Common Law: Gordon Tullock's Critique." *Public Choice* 135: 35–53.

Printed in the United States
By Bookmasters